Recipes for Great Canadian Weekends

FROM HOLIDAY INNS

A TRIBUTE TO THE TRAVELLER

Copyright 1987 Commonwealth Holiday Inns of Canada Limited

Published by Commonwealth Holiday Inns of Canada Limited

First Printing 1987

ISBN NO. 0-9692821-0-9

Cover and food photography – Pat LaCroix, The Brant Group
Stylist – Deborah Messal
Food Stylist – Olga Truchan

Production – House of Housden Inc.
Graphic Design – Jennie Clark
Design Associates – Dave Johnson, Lynette Long
Calligraphy – Ann Housden
Illustrations – Renée Mansfield

Recipe Copy – Nancy Smallwood
Editor – Winnie Czulinski
Recipes by Members of the Holiday Inns Culinary Olympic Teams

PHOTOGRAPHY CREDITS
Michael Assaly, pages 6, 7
Rawl Furman, page 8
Pat LaCroix, page 12 (Ontario and Quebec Editions)

THE IMAGE BANK CANADA
      DC Productions, page 14 (Western Edition)
      Brett Froomer, page 12 (Prairies Edition)
      Gary Crallé, page 14 (Prairies Edition)
      Marc Romanelli, page 14 (Ontario & Quebec Editions)
      Hans Wendler, page 12 (Western and Atlantic Editions)
      Gary Crallé, page 14 (Atlantic Edition)

Printed and bound in Canada by Friesen Printers,
on 100 lb. Jenson Gloss, Provincial Papers

Table of Contents

This book is dedicated to the millions of travellers who set out each year to find their own bit of Canada ~ some of its beauty and challenge, some of its peace and solitude, some of its culture, history and sport.

The call to travel and the urge to see new sights are difficult to ignore. We know you take pride in the roots you've put down for yourself and loved ones, but we also know about that wanderlust that won't be stilled. That's our business. You'd like to experience something else and you can. Wherever you live in Canada, you have the world at your feet. This world, our country, is one of unceasing contrast that may beckon to you with its very strangeness or lure you with its variety.

We know you love and appreciate the good life – travel, culture, photography, entertainment and art. Within these pages we hope you'll discover a destination or landmark that may become a favourite. We've included some of the most popular sights and events and also some of the lesser-known.

Here, too, are some special dishes for you. They're your favourites. That's what our Canada-wide research in Holiday Inn Hotel restaurants tells us. We hope you'll enjoy preparing them in your home. Of course, we'd also like to see you stay with us and let us prepare some for you.

With the following descriptions and recipes, we've tried to present the best places to visit and some of your favourite weekend fare.

Bon voyage and bon appetit !

Our Story

We at Commonwealth Holiday Inns of Canada recently celebrated our Silver Anniversary. In 1962, we opened our first Canadian hotel in London, Ontario. Today, twenty-five years later, we are the nation's largest hotel chain, with fifty-six Holiday Inn Hotels coast to coast (and ten in the United Kingdom), and some twelve thousand guest rooms.

Our book, RECIPES FOR GREAT CANADIAN WEEKENDS, is a tribute to you, our guest. After all, we owe our success and growth to you.

We appreciate your loyalty and we'll do everything we can to keep you coming back again and again. Whether you're staying with us in British Columbia or Newfoundland, our concern is for your satisfaction, comfort and pleasure. We have ten thousand dedicated men and women to cater to your needs.

Staying with us on business? We have superb meeting and conference facilities. Our experienced staff will arrange full-scale conventions or smaller meetings, receptions, formal dinners, or theme parties designed for your individual needs. We also provide secretarial, photocopying and telex facilities, and the very latest state-of-the-art audiovisual equipment, including simultaneous translation.

Your health and fitness is of equal concern to us. That's why we're setting up a network of fully equipped Fitness Centres across the country. We have testing labs, weight rooms, squash and tennis courts, saunas, steam rooms, whirlpools and aerobics studios, all managed by highly qualified Fitness Directors. These facilities are available free to registered guests and at very competitive fees to local members. As further proof of our concern for your healthier lifestyle, we offer nutritionally balanced menus, alcohol-free drinks, fitness breaks (for livelier meetings), aquabics sessions, jogging routes, and in some cases, skipping ropes on the room service menu.

Many of our hotels are situated in city centres for your convenience, whether you're on business, shopping, or taking in the cultural sights. Other Holiday Inn Hotels are strategically located in smaller communities, with easy access from major highways.

At the end of a tiring day comfort is important to you. Our rooms are spacious, and all equipped with double or king sized beds. Many of our hotels feature rooms with pant pressers, hair dryers, remote control colour televisions, in-house movies and mini-bars. Soft drink and ice dispensers are available to all our guests.

We want you and your family to feel at home. Children are always welcome and stay and eat (from their own special menu) free of charge when they share accommodation with their parents.

Yes, we're proud of our hotels and pleased we've been able to serve travellers from around the world these past twenty-five years. The world's most advanced reservation system of its kind, the Holiday Inn system, will ensure your room is waiting in more than seventeen hundred hotels in over fifty countries around the globe. (For reservations, dial 1-800-HOLIDAY.)

In an effort to maintain our leading role on the Canadian hotel scene, we offer you the finest in regional and international cuisine in our restaurants. This is a cuisine befitting an industry leader in Canada. More important, it is a cuisine aimed to please your palate.

Our Culinary Teams

*A*s a trendsetter in the accommodation industry and the company against which others measure their success, Holiday Inn strives for excellence in all areas. In keeping with this dedication, we have created two culinary teams who compete both nationally and internationally against the world's best. Team members are also fully involved in the creation of menus, recipes, training, research and development projects and the identification of today's trends.

Our Culinary Teams have had some dramatic international successes at the World Culinary Olympics in Frankfurt and the 1986 World Cup Competition in Luxembourg. Both individual and team efforts resulted in five Gold, Silver and Bronze awards in all categories, including Hors d'Oeuvres, Entrées, Pastries and Petits Fours.

We are proud of our teams, which are comprised of some of Canada's most exacting and creative chefs. They're equally proud of their achievements and so they should be. Now you have a chance to sample some of the fine foods of their labours. You'll see and taste these high standards in the quality, variety and value of the dishes offered in our restaurants across Canada.

* Vancouver's Chinatown is the second largest in North America.

* The Bay of Fundy in New Brunswick has the highest tides in the world.

* Regina is the home of the Royal Canadian Mounted Police.

* Many Holiday Inn Hotel rooms have hairdryers, pant pressers and remote control TVs.

* The longest white sand beach in Canada is on Lesser Slave Lake in Alberta.

* Many Holiday Inn Hotels have a resident Fitness Director to assist guests and members in their fitness programs.

* Holiday Inn Hotels have special programs designed for sporting groups.

* Holiday Inn Hotels import many fine wines to Canada and are available at very reasonable prices.

* Speedy check out service is now available in all Holiday Inn Hotels across Canada.

* Holiflex is Holiday Inn Hotels' own fitness system available at most of the hotels across the country.

* Holiday Inn Hotels have great programs for senior citizens.

* Holiday Inn Hotels have a program called Great Rates that provide super low rates for many weekends and some holidays.

* The Rideau Canal in Ottawa is the World's Longest Skating rink.

* The Holiday Inn Hotels' reservation system is the most advanced system in the world.

* Montreal is the second largest French-speaking city in the world.

* The first transatlantic wireless signal was received in St. John's, Newfoundland.

* The first permanent European settlement in Canada was Port Royal, Nova Scotia in 1605.

* Many Holiday Inn Hotels have memberships in local tennis, squash and racquet clubs for use by their guests.

Travellers' Trivia

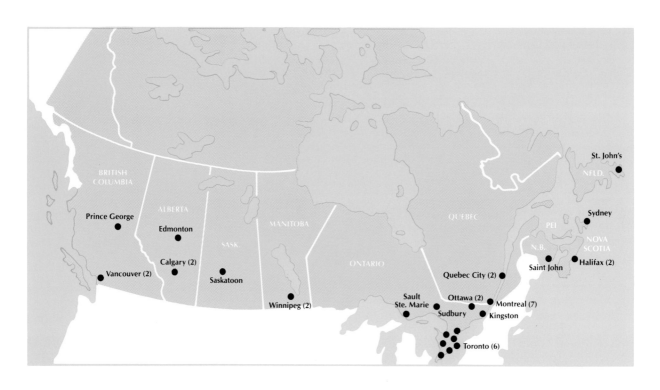

HOLIDAY INNS IN CANADA

BRITISH COLUMBIA

Prince George . . . . (604) 563-0055
Vancouver Broadway . . . . . . (604) 879-0511
Vancouver Harbourside . . . . (604) 689-9211

ALBERTA

Calgary Downtown . . . . (403) 263-7600
Calgary MacLeod Trail . . . . . (403) 287-2700
Edmonton . . . . (403) 429-2861

SASKATCHEWAN

Saskatoon . . . . (306) 244-2311

MANITOBA

Winnipeg Downtown . . . . . . (204) 942-0551
Winnipeg South . . . . (204) 452-4747

ONTARIO

Barrie . . . . (705) 728-6191
Brampton . . . . (416) 792-9900
Brantford . . . . (519) 753-8651
Burlington . . . . (416) 639-4443
Cambridge . . . . (519) 658-4601
Cornwall . . . . (613) 933-8000

Guelph . . . . (519) 836-0231
Hamilton . . . . (416) 528-3451
Kingston . . . . (613) 549-8400
Kitchener . . . . (519) 893-1211
London City Centre . . . . (519) 439-1661
Orillia . . . . (705) 325-9511
Oshawa . . . . (416) 576-5101
Ottawa Centre . . . . (613) 238-1122
Ottawa Market Square . . . . . (613) 236-0201
Owen Sound . . . . (519) 376-1551
Peterborough . . . . (705) 743-1144
St. Catharines . . . . (416) 934-2561
Sarnia . . . . (519) 336-4130
Sault Ste. Marie . . . . (705) 949-0611
Sudbury . . . . (705) 675-1123
Toronto Airport . . . . (416) 675-7611
Toronto Don Valley . . . . (416) 449-4111
Toronto Downtown . . . . (416) 977-0707
Toronto Etobicoke . . . . (416) 621-2121
Toronto Scarborough . . . . . . (416) 293-8171
Toronto Yorkdale . . . . (416) 789-5161
Windsor . . . . (519) 253-4411

QUEBEC

Montreal Downtown . . . . . . (514) 842-6111
Montreal Le Seville . . . . (514) 332-2720
Montreal Longueuil . . . . (514) 670-3030

Montreal Place Dupuis . . . . . (514) 842-4881
Montreal Pointe Claire . . . . . (514) 697-7110
Montreal Richelieu . . . . (514) 842-8581
Montreal Seigneurie . . . . (514) 731-7751
Quebec City Downtown . . . . (418) 647-2611
Quebec City Ste. Foy . . . . . . (418) 653-4901

NOVA SCOTIA

Halifax Centre . . . . (902) 423-1161
Halifax Dartmouth . . . . (902) 463-1100
Sydney . . . . (902) 539-6750

NEW BRUNSWICK

Saint John City Centre . . . . . (506) 657-3610

NEWFOUNDLAND

Clarenville . . . . (709) 466-7911
Gander . . . . (709) 256-3981
St. John's . . . . (709) 722-0506
St. John's Crowne Plaza . . . . (709) 739-6404

HOLIDAY INN TOLL FREE NUMBER

(800) HOLIDAY   (800) 465-4329

O Canada! What an incredible country! We have over five thousand miles from Victoria, British Columbia to St. John's, Newfoundland and two thousand five hundred miles from the North Pole to the U.S. border. Three ocean-swept coasts outline a land rich with endless variety.

There are the mountains, older than time, that still shelter a multitude of wildlife, as do our forests. Our trees are one of our most valued resources. They're as much a constant of Canada as the sun-baked, winter-pummelled prairies where no trees may grow, but where camaraderie and pride thrive like the hardiest strain of wheat. There are also countless unspoiled rivers and lakes, many surrounded by natural trails and close to Holiday Inn Hotels.

And then there is the other Canada, the Canada we have made. This includes our industries, our towns and our cities – clean, cosmopolitan and safe, where cultures and manmade achievements soon blend to leave impressions more lasting than photographs.

Canada's people make this huge nation unique. From the west coast Haida Indians to down-Easterners with a lilt of the Irish or Scottish, from the Mennonite and Amish to the Italian and Chinese, they, and we, have come to stay. See it on your next weekend, perhaps, in the throbbing Saturday markets that are the colour and life of a melting pot of nations come to mean "Canadian."

All this and more is waiting for you to discover. We've called our book RECIPES FOR GREAT CANADIAN WEEKENDS for two reasons. Of course we'd like you to spend some of your weekends at home trying our recipes. We've made them easy to follow and as irresistible as we can. But when you want to get away from the hot stove and home pressures…come and stay with us. Here, you'll find some destinations and diversions that may become your favourites. Eat, discover and enjoy!

Your Great Canadian Weekend

Canada's Centre of Commerce

Ontario was once covered with a mountain system, still seen today in the rocky upland known as the Canadian Shield. This hardly begins to describe the province. Besides nickel mines and the Great Lakes, you will find some of the richest and softest farmland in Canada. Ontario is also the mist and thunder of Niagara Falls, endless pine forests, maples stained crimson and the ghosts of Loyalists and Jesuit missionaries.

Ottawa is Canada's capital city and home of the Federal Government. Dubbed Canada's Westminster and beautifully set among the Gatineau Hills, it is intersected by the Rideau Canal, in winter the world's largest skating rink. Here, too, is the Peace Tower, in memory of Canadians killed during World War One. Within sight of Ottawa's Parliament Buildings you will find Gatineau Park, scenic enough in any season and an unforgettable blaze of colour in autumn.

Two hundred miles west is Toronto, Ontario's provincial capital. This city is a cultural metropolis of three million people reflected in Metro's International Caravan Festival held each year. Immigrants have brought both colour and economy to a once staid city, while architects have transformed the skyline into towers of steel, glass and shimmering gold. The Toronto Stock Exchange is one of the world's largest, handling over two-thirds of Canada's trading volume.

A good way to orient yourself in this waterfront city is to start out from Toronto's New and Old City Halls, at Bay and Queen Streets. The contrast of the buildings' architecture – ultra-modern and gloriously Gothic – is indicative of the city itself.

Laurier House

This 1870s stone mansion in Ottawa was the residence of two Canadian Prime Ministers – Sir Wilfred Laurier and Mackenzie King. You can see the study, dining room, bedroom and the recreation of Lester B. Pearson's library. There's a wealth of furniture (including one or two late-medieval items), documents, photographs – and the crystal ball Mackenzie King used at his seances.

Nepean Point Park

Here, you can relax from your Ottawa sightseeing and enjoy the view – of the Gothic towers and blocks of Parliament Hill behind you and the city of Hull, Quebec, across the river. There's an amphitheatre for summer concerts and plays and a statue of the French explorer, Samuel de Champlain.

Ontario Science Centre

Actually built into the side of a hill and designed to ravine contours, this Toronto building is called the museum of the twenty-first century. It houses more than five hundred intriguing hands-on, push-button exhibits, theatres with film and slide shows and a film library. This is just the place to discover worlds ranging from the inner workings of a TV studio to electrical storms. Try the static electricity machine to make your hair (literally) stand on end.

CN Tower

This is the world's tallest freestanding structure – at eighteen hundred and fifteen feet twice as high as the Eiffel Tower. Glass-walled elevators whisk you up steel and reinforced concrete to eleven hundred and thirty-six feet above the city. On a clear day you can see up to seventy-five miles around you. The tower pod has broadcasting facilities, indoor and outdoor observation decks and another elevator to the space deck above. Back on ground floor there's a futuristic games area, with a thrilling simulated space experience, "Tour of the Universe."

Fort York

Founded by Lieutenant-Governor Simcoe, this restored 1793 fort recaptures some of the city's stirring history. It was a defence base in the 1812 war; here, in 1813, seventeen hundred Americans defeated seven hundred Toronto defenders. Those left of the latter promptly set fire to the fort's gunpowder supply, the Grand Magazine, to prevent American takeover of the base. Today, you can see the Fort York Guard, in early nineteenth century uniform, performing drills and letting off muskets and cannon. You can also walk through the buildings – some containing officers' and soldiers' quarters – to see everything from models, maps and uniforms to equipment and tools.

Destinations for Weekend Wanderers

TORONTO

Harbourfront, an ultramodern shopping and entertainment centre.

Ontario Place, an entertainment complex on three manmade islands in Lake Ontario. Includes children's playground, theatres and Future Pod Showcase with the latest in high-tech.

The CN Tower, the world's tallest freestanding structure, with observation decks and futuristic games base.

Royal Ontario Museum. From dinosaurs to Ming Tombs.

Ontario Science Centre. An absolute must for the family.

Art Gallery of Ontario, with the world's largest Henry Moore Collection.

George R. Gardiner Museum of Ceramic Art. A beautiful collection of ceramics.

Toronto Islands, a pleasant ferry ride away.

Scarborough Bluffs, ninety-metre hills rising over Lake Ontario.

Metropolitan Zoo, one of the world's finest.

Casa Loma, a ninety-eight room turreted "castle."

Woodbine Race Track. Thoroughbred racing and home of the Queen's Plate.

OTTAWA

Parliament Buildings. Three massive Victorian buildings, extensively rebuilt after a 1916 fire. See also the Centre Block with Peace Tower and multi-bell carillon, and Memorial Chamber.

Canadian War Museum, for Canada's military history.
National Arts Centre, with opera house, theatre and studio.
Museum of Canadian Scouting.
Centennial Experimental Farm.
National Museum of Science and Technology with hands-on exhibits.
The National Gallery, with Canada's largest art collection.
Royal Canadian Mint.
Sparks Street Mall. Shopping, art exhibitions and gardens.
National Library and Public Archives.
Notre-Dame Basilica (1841).
Changing of the Guard, daily on Parliament Hill during the summer.
Central Canada Exhibition, August.
Slide-A-Ride, three hundred and fifty-foot long flume (water-ride) south on Highway 31.

OTHER PLACES
Canada's Wonderland. A three hundred and twenty-acre theme park with Hanna-
  Barbera Land, Salt Water Circus, street entertainers, and much more. North of Toronto.
Niagara-on-the-Lake, original capital of Upper Canada and home of the Shaw
  Festival.
Stratford and the Shakespeare Festival.
Upper Canada Village, Morrisburg.
Sainte-Marie-among-the-Hurons, Midland, a Jesuit missionary site.
Serpent Mounds Provincial Park, south of Peterborough.
Old Fort Henry, Kingston (Canada's military college).

Ontario's Best in Food and Drink

Cheese, especially Cheddar.
Honey.
Fruits and vegetables from the Niagara Belt and Holland Marsh, and regional
  delights like Niagara Apple Betty (pudding).
Maple syrup and maple products.
Ontario lamb.
Products from wineries and cottage breweries.

To Buy

Native arts and crafts, from wood carvings to buckskin.
Mennonite and Amish crafts, including quilts and "apple dolls" (novelties fashioned
  out of wizened apples).
Semi-precious stones and minerals (quartz, fool's gold).
Ontario pine furniture.
Maple products.

Clam Chowder

This hearty soup full of nutrition is a good winter weekend lunch choice. It's also a colourful addition to a dinner menu.

ingredients

1½ oz. each chopped celery, English cucumber, onion, red and green pepper

2 Tbsp. butter

1 cup cooked cubed potatoes

2 oz. flour

5 oz. can clams with juice

2½ cups 2% milk

1 bay leaf

Salt and pepper to taste

Dash paprika & thyme

2 strips cooked bacon, diced

Red pepper and parsley (optional)

directions

Sauté vegetables, except potatoes, in 2 Tbsp. butter for 2 to 3 minutes. Add flour and stir well until absorbed into butter. Pour in milk slowly and simmer, covered, for 20 minutes. Add cooked cubed potatoes, clams and juice, salt, pepper and bay leaf. Simmer for an additional 10 minutes (do not boil). Garnish with strips of red pepper and parsley if desired.

Makes 4 servings ~ 175 calories per serving

Tempting Trio

Also a time-honoured trio, these soups are favourites for more than their taste ~ they're easy to prepare.

Chicken Noodle Soup

In a 2 quart saucepan, sauté 2 oz. each of celery, onions and carrots in 2 Tbsp. butter until tender (approx. 5 mins.). Pour in 5 cups chicken stock and bring to the boil. Add 1 cup diced cooked chicken, 3/4 cup uncooked noodles, salt and pepper and simmer for 10 minutes.

Makes 6 servings ~ 104 calories per serving

Cream of Tomato Soup

In a 2 quart saucepan, sauté 1 oz. each of diced celery and carrots and 2½ oz. each of chopped onions and fresh tomatoes in 2 Tbsp. butter until tender (approx. 5 mins.). Add 2 Tbsp. flour to absorb butter and stir for 3 to 4 minutes. Pour in 4 cups chicken stock, add 1¼ cups tomato purée, 1 bay leaf and pinch of thyme. Cover and simmer for 45 minutes, then strain soup. Turn off heat and stir in 1 cup of half-and-half cream.

Makes 6 servings ~ 133 calories per serving

Beef Vegetable Soup

In a 2 quart saucepan, sauté 2 oz. each of chopped onion, carrot, celery, broccoli and cauliflower until tender (approx. 5 mins.). Pour in 4½ cups beef stock. Add 1 small chopped tomato, 1 bay leaf, pinch of thyme and simmer for 10 minutes. Add 6 oz. diced cooked fresh beef and 1 oz. white wine (if desired). Season and simmer for 5 minutes.

Makes 6 servings ~ 110 calories per serving

Goulash Soup

Here's a soup that's almost a stew and has a way of becoming a meal in itself. We recommend top sirloin butt, but any cut of beef will do, including lean ground beef.

ingredients

1 Tbsp. vegetable oil

4 oz. top sirloin butt, finely chopped

2 oz. tomato paste

1 oz. paprika

½ cup cooking onions, diced

1 garlic clove, finely chopped

¼ cup each red and green pepper

4 cups beef stock

1 bay leaf

Dash marjoram

Pinch caraway seeds, salt and pepper

½ cup diced potatoes

1 Tbsp. sour cream

directions

Sauté beef in vegetable oil until lightly browned. Add tomato paste and paprika, onion, garlic and peppers. Simmer, stirring for 2 to 3 minutes. Pour in beef stock, add bay leaf, marjoram, caraway seeds, salt and pepper and let simmer for 30 mins. Add potatoes to the last 15 minutes cooking time. Stir in sour cream just before serving

Makes 6 servings ~ 118 calories per serving

Minestrone Soup

Here's an Italian standard Canadians love and with good reason; it's festive with colour and full of nutrition. Italian sausage gives it extra zest. Our minestrone also improves with age ~ it tastes even better the second day.

ingredients

2 Tbsp. butter

1 medium onion, chopped

2 garlic cloves, crushed

¾ lb. Italian sausage, sliced or chopped

½ cup each chopped carrots, celery and green pepper

16 oz. can tomatoes

4 cups chicken stock

10 oz. can kidney beans

1 cup uncooked noodles (any kind)

Salt and black pepper to taste

directions

In a 4 quart saucepan, sauté onion and garlic in butter. Add sausage and remaining ingredients except noodles and simmer for ¾ hour. Put noodles in and simmer for an additional 10 minutes.

note:
Carrots, celery and kidney beans are traditional but not 'de rigueur' for minestrone. Other firm vegetables such as broccoli work well.

Makes 6 servings ~ 324 calories per serving

Cream of Mushroom Soup

Thick, warming and delicious, this is destined to become a cold-weather classic. Our combination of beef and chicken stocks gives it that extra-rich taste.

ingredients

1 lb. fresh mushrooms

3 oz. butter

2 oz. flour

2½ cups beef stock

2½ cups chicken stock

1 cup half-and-half cream

Salt and pepper to taste

Chives (optional)

directions

Wash, trim and slice mushrooms. In a 2 quart saucepan sauté mushrooms in butter for 5 minutes until just golden. Add flour to absorb butter and stir for 2 to 3 minutes. Pour in stock add salt and pepper and turn off heat. Stir in cream and garnish with chives for a soup that looks as good as it tastes.

Makes 6 servings ~ 242 calories per serving

French Onion Soup

That delectable cheesy topping is a sure lure ~ to a wealth of beef and onion flavour steaming beneath.

Ingredients

3 Tbsp. butter
1½ lbs. onions, sliced
6 cups beef stock
1 bay leaf
Pinch thyme
Salt and pepper to taste
3 oz. white wine

Topping:
12 oz. Emmenthal cheese, grated
6 oz. Parmesan cheese
6 slices French bread

Directions

In a 4 quart saucepan sauté sliced onions in butter until transparent (not brown). Add stock, bay leaf, thyme, salt and pepper and simmer for 30 minutes. Pour in white wine and simmer an additional 15 minutes. Divide soup into 6 ovenware soup bowls and place 1 slice French bread on each. Sprinkle 2 oz. Emmenthal cheese over each slice and top with Parmesan. Brown under broiler.

Note:
Cutting up onions can be a teary task, but doing them in the sink under running cold water helps; so does a sharp knife.

Makes 6 generous servings ~ 537 calories per serving

Tossed Salad

Low in calories and high in vitamins, minerals and iron, a tossed salad is nutrition at its best.

Diversify your base with different lettuces ~ head or iceberg (that tight-leaved standard); leaf (crisp and curly); romaine (an elongated leaf with nutty flavour); Boston (smooth and "buttery"); endive (a broad, light-to-dark green leaf with almost bitter taste). Spinach, loaded with iron, is a good addition, while watercress adds a pleasant bite.

Lettuce should be washed and patted or drained dry, or dried in a spinner. Tear lettuce leaves into bite-sized pieces to fill your salad bowl.

Unpeeled cucumber adds contrast; for more colour add radish pieces and shredded or coined carrots. Line up celery stalks and cut pieces all at once. Mushrooms, neatly sliced are an attractive addition. Other possibilities include broccoli, cauliflower, red or green onion, bean and alfalfa sprouts and red and green pepper. Add tomato slices at the last moment to prevent their "bleeding" over greens.

Toss with your favourite dressing, if desired, and add garnishes, such as chopped egg, cheese and croutons, just before serving.

Caesar Salad

The Emperor of salads is not difficult to prepare. It merely requires a little organization to have all dressing ingredients assembled just before serving time.

ingredients

1 head romaine lettuce

2 garlic cloves

1 anchovy fillet

2 egg yolks

Dash onion mustard

1 Tbsp. lemon juice

½ tsp. freshly ground pepper

½ tsp. Worcestershire Sauce

1 tsp. salt

4 oz. olive oil

Garlic croutons, Parmesan cheese, bacon bits

directions

Wash romaine, discard outside leaves and tear into bite-sized pieces. Dry, wrap in paper towels and refrigerate. In a wooden bowl crush garlic cloves and anchovy fillet to make a paste. Beat egg yolks and add to garlic paste. Add all other ingredients except oil and mix well. Just before serving, blend oil slowly into mixture and stir. Toss in lettuce, top with croutons, Parmesan cheese and bacon bits and serve.

Makes 6 servings ~ 269 calories per serving

Fruit Platter

This healthy offering can be a thing of beauty too. Begin with a focal point ~ a centrepiece of one particular fruit, or a bowl of yogurt, sherbet or cottage cheese, whipped or sour cream.

You can use iceberg lettuce as a "bed" of overlapping leaves, or as individual nests to hold fruit. For sturdier containers try the shells of pineapple, melon, grapefruit or orange.

Think "variety" with exotic fruits like papaya, persimmon or passionfruit. Also, dark fruits like black Ribier grapes make a striking contrast to paler fruit. Try alternating balls of honeydew and canteloupe melon. Watermelon wedges make good dividers for your fruit platter.

Slice bananas diagonally and add just before serving. To prevent any sliced fruit from browning, dip in lemon, lime, grapefruit or pineapple juice.

Don't forget iron-rich dried fruits, or perhaps an assort~ ment of nuts and cheeses. For the finishing touch, try a garnish of pineapple leaves, fresh mint sprigs, crushed wal~ nuts, a dusting of cinnamon ~ or frosted mint leaves. Dip in beaten egg white and granulated sugar ~ arrange ~ and anticipate compliments.

Julienne Salad

Presented properly and in a glass or china bowl, this salad is a striking dish. It's the combination of colours and arrangement of ingredients that make it so special.

ingredients

1 head of iceberg lettuce
2 oz. each of Swiss cheese, Black Forest ham and turkey breast
1 each: cherry tomato, hard-cooked egg and radish
2 each: black olives, green olives and red onion rings
Alfalfa sprouts for garnish

directions

Line two bowls with whole lettuce leaves. Chop remainder of lettuce and pile in centre of each bowl. Cut cheese, ham and turkey into ½" wide strips and arrange on lettuce. Add other ingredients artistically around bowl, and garnish with alfalfa sprouts.

note:
Whole wheat rolls make this a well-rounded meal, according to Canada's Food Guide. Relatively low in calories and full of energy, it's a delicious change for lunch or dinner.

Makes 2 servings ~ 311 calories per serving

Shrimp Cocktail

It isn't every day you serve your guests a treat like this ~ so don't skimp on shrimp size! Proper shrimp bowls, too, are best for this appetizer, but a clear stemmed glass, white wine goblet or even a fruit nappy also work well.

To prepare: Shred lettuce and fill glass ¾ full. Meanwhile, place shrimp, allowing 5 per person, in boiling water with 1 tsp. salt and 1 bay leaf. Bring water back to boil, turn off heat and allow shrimp to stand in water for 3 minutes. Cool immediately under cold running water and drain.

Peel shrimp, leaving tail on and remove back vein. Hang individually on the side of glass or bowl.

Prepared seafood sauce can be found at any grocery store, but here's a quick and tasty homemade offering: Combine 1 Tbsp. ketchup, 1 Tbsp. chili sauce, a dash each of Worcestershire sauce and Tabasco, 1 tsp. horseradish and 1 Tbsp. lemon juice for each serving. Scoop into centre of dish over lettuce and garnish with a wedge of lemon.

Refrigerate until serving time

125 calories per serving

Reuben Sandwich

This is an impressive lunchtime sandwich ~ a restaurant favourite, but not one many people think of preparing at home. In fact, it's as simple to prepare as most other toasted sandwiches (and the ingredients keep for at least a week, covered, in the refrigerator). For an even richer sandwich, dip the rye bread in egg and fry lightly in butter.

ingredients

Have your butcher slice the corned beef very thinly. For each sandwich use:

1 slice rye bread ~ ½ oz. butter   3 oz. sauerkraut

3 oz. corned beef   2 oz. Swiss cheese

directions

Wrap the corned beef in foil and heat through ~ about 5 mins. at 300° in the oven. Sauerkraut should be heated in the same manner. If using vacuum-packed corned beef, follow package directions and place sauerkraut in top half of double boiler to heat through. Place corned beef on one slice of buttered toast or fried rye bread. Top with sauerkraut and Swiss cheese. Melt under broiler and serve.

Makes a single serving ~ 650 calories per sandwich

Club
Sandwich

One of the most popular sandwiches in North America ~ and we think we know why. It's nutritious ~ chock-full of protein, vitamins, minerals and carbohydrates, filling but not heavy ~ and it's an entire meal that can be eaten with the fingers!

The authentic club is made as follows:

Butter one side each of 3 slices of toast (white, brown or rye). Spread mayonnaise on one slice, top with lettuce and slices of cooked turkey or chicken. Top with second slice of toast. Add 3 slices of tomato and 3 slices of bacon to second slice, top with lettuce and finish with third slice of toast.

Secure the four corners with fancy toothpicks and cut sandwich into quarters. Garnish with a cherry tomato and alfalfa sprouts.

note:
As there is a fair amount of work to these sandwiches, we suggest the assembly line method ~ that of making 4 sandwiches, one layer at a time. The toast may cool off in the process, but popping the finished product into the oven for 3 to 4 minutes will freshen things up.

Makes 1 serving ~ 584 calories per serving

French Dip

Yesterday's roast beef can have new life as a main course today (although we favour a fresh roast). Before you add flour to roasting pan drippings for that perfect gravy, set aside ½ cup of the drippings for au jus sandwiches, and refrigerate overnight.

Heat 1 cup of water to boiling, then add 1 bouillon cube, salt and pepper and the ½ cup of drippings.

Meanwhile, slice roast beef as thinly as possible, place in ovenproof covered dish to prevent drying and heat through at 300° for about 5 minutes.

Slice lengthwise and then in half a really fresh French stick. Butter both sides and arrange roast beef on top. Cover with second slice.

Pour the au jus in individual small bowls. Serve with condiments such as mustard, mayonnaise and horseradish.

note:
Freeze any leftover "au jus" and add to your next pot of onion or minestrone soup.

Makes 4 "au jus" servings

Hot Ham and Cheese Croissant

The croissant ~ it's one of the best things since sliced bread and much more elegant! To really do it justice, eat it on its own, or reserve it for the finest fillings. The possibilities for croissant sandwiches are many, but they should, according to the French, always be served hot.

Black Forest Ham makes a delectable croissant filling and with the addition of Swiss cheese ~ a gastronomic delight and one of the most popular lunchtime or entrée sandwiches.

Have your butcher slice the ham very thinly. A small heap of folded ham is much more pleasing than a single flat slice. The Swiss cheese, too, should be thinly sliced, rather than grated.

We suggest you heat the croissant first. Split it and fill with two or three slices of the ham and one or two slices of Swiss cheese. Return to the oven for 2 minutes to melt cheese.

Serve with a piece of cantaloupe ~ a nice contrast, or with a bowl of one of our tasty soups.

note:
You might like to try these other fillings; salmon and tomato; avocado and pepperoni; smoked salmon and cream cheese.

Serves one ~ 489 calories per serving

Hamburger

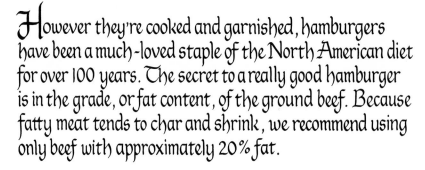

However they're cooked and garnished, hamburgers have been a much-loved staple of the North American diet for over 100 years. The secret to a really good hamburger is in the grade, or fat content, of the ground beef. Because fatty meat tends to char and shrink, we recommend using only beef with approximately 20% fat.

Season 1 lb. of ground beef with salt and pepper and form into patties. Broil approximately 6 minutes per side for "well done". Serve on a Kaiser roll topped with your choice of lettuce, tomato slices, onions, fried mushrooms and cheddar cheese. Serve with mustard, relish, ketchup and dill pickles.

note:
If you like your hamburger buns hard outside and soft in the middle, heat, unsliced, in a 300° oven for 4 minutes. Prefer them all soft? Place in a brown paper bag, seal, and sprinkle generously with water before placing them in the oven. For buns with a crunch, simply split and toast under the broiler.

Makes 4 to 6 servings ~ 365 calories per serving

Western Omelette

Intimidated by the perfect omelette? Don't be. The secret, for that desired fluffiness, is not to overcook the eggs.

ingredients

3 eggs per serving ~ 2 Tbsp. butter

2 Tbsp. each of diced ham, onions and red and green peppers (previously cooked together and kept on low heat)

Salt and pepper to taste

Cherry tomato and alfalfa sprouts (optional)

directions

Beat eggs in a bowl with salt and pepper. Melt 2 Tbsp. butter in a medium skillet, until frothy. Add egg mixture and lightly scramble. When nearly cooked, fold the omelette and transfer to a serving plate. Slit the centre of the omelette open and fill with the cooked ham, onions and red and green peppers. Garnish with cherry tomato and alfalfa sprouts, if desired. Serve omelette with toast, rolls and butter, or a small tossed salad.

Makes 1 serving ~ 462 calories per serving

Fish and Chips

The key to really good fish and chips is the fish batter and the heat of the oil. We recommend using cod, but any fresh fish fillet (except salmon or trout) is excellent batter-fried.

ingredients

4 pieces of cod fillet, 4 oz. each ~ 4 medium potatoes

Batter:

4 oz. flour   Dash salt and pepper

1 tsp. baking powder   1 cup water

directions

Combine all batter ingredients and mix well. If lumps remain, strain batter. Let stand for 15 minutes before coating fish.

Meanwhile, peel and cut 4 medium potatoes into chips. Soak in warm water 5 minutes to remove excess starch. Drain and pat dry. Roll cod fillets in seasoned flour to coat well and dip in batter. Deep fry at 350° for 6 minutes until golden brown. Drain on paper towels and keep warm.

Deep fry potatoes until golden brown and drain on paper towels. Serve with wedge of lemon and/or tartar sauce. Garnish with cherry tomato and alfalfa sprouts if desired.

Makes 4 servings ~ 429 calories per serving

Shrimp Stir Fry

Like vegetable soup, a stir fry can include all those vegetables in your refrigerator. Because they're cooked only to the "al dente" (crisp-tender) stage, vegetables retain their colour and flavour, making this dish both attractive and delicious.

ingredients

8 large shrimp cut in 3 (or 12 medium cut in half)

½ cup each of 4 fresh vegetables* cut diagonally

1 garlic clove, chopped

1 oz. sesame oil, 1 oz. soy sauce

¼ cup chicken stock

½ oz. cornstarch

½ tsp. fresh ginger

directions

Heat ½ of sesame oil in a large frying pan or wok and sauté shrimp, stirring constantly for 2 minutes or until cooked. Remove from pan and set aside. Add remaining ½ oz. sesame oil to pan and add vegetables (harder ones first) one at a time. Sauté for 3 minutes and add garlic and ginger. Mix chicken stock and cornstarch to make a paste, stir in soy sauce. Add to vegetables. Return shrimp to pan and stir fry 1 minute more to mix well. Serve as is, or over rice.

* Choice of vegetables: carrots, cauliflower, broccoli, celery, onions, mushrooms, snow peas, zucchini, Chinese cabbage, red and green peppers.

Makes 2 servings ~ 238 calories per serving

Beef Stir Fry

For the very best beef stir fry, we recommend tenderloin. However, you can use other steaks such as rib, wing, T-bone or sirloin. These are less expensive and easier to cut in strips, Chinese-style.

ingredients

8 oz. beef tenderloin cut in ½" strips

¼ cup each of 4 fresh vegetables* cut diagonally

1 garlic clove, chopped

1 oz. sesame oil, 1 oz. soy sauce

¼ cup beef stock

½ oz. cornstarch

½ tsp. fresh ginger

directions

Heat ½ of sesame oil in large frying pan or wok. Sauté beef, stirring constantly until cooked (about 2 minutes). Remove from pan and set aside. Add remaining ½ oz. sesame oil to pan, then add vegetables, harder ones first, one at a time. Sauté for 3 minutes and add garlic and ginger.

Mix beef stock and cornstarch to make a paste, stir in soy sauce. Add to vegetables and stir. Return beef to pan and stir fry for 1 minute more to mix well. Serve as is, or over rice.

*Choice of vegetables: carrots, cauliflower, broccoli, celery, onions, mushrooms, snow peas, zucchini, Chinese cabbage, red and green peppers.

Makes 2 servings ~ 407 calories per serving.

Fettuccine di Mare

With pasta, almost anything is possible. There are many varieties of noodles and sauce and even more ways of putting them together.

ingredients

seafood sauce mixture:
½ lb. sole fillets
1 oz. white wine
2 Tbsp. finely diced onion
¼ cup baby shrimp
¼ cup baby scallops
¼ cup mussels
Salt and pepper to taste

pasta:
4 cups cooked noodles
2 Tbsp. butter
1 garlic clove, minced
1 cup 35% cream
1 tsp. Parmesan cheese
Mussels in the shell (Optional)

directions

Place all seafood sauce ingredients in top of double boiler and poach until fish is tender (about 10 mins.). Divide mixture in two. Purée one half and reserve balance for topping. Set aside.

Cook noodles in boiling salted water to which 1 tsp. oil has been added. When noodles are "al dente" remove from heat. Drain and rinse.

Heat 2 Tbsp. butter in pan. Sauté onion and garlic until transparent, then add cooked fettuccine noodles and toss. Pour in fish purée and toss; add cream, Parmesan cheese and remaining flaked fish and heat through. Divide into 4 portions & garnish with mussels in shell.

Makes 4 servings ~ 525 calories per serving

Fettuccine Alfredo

This is the most loved fettuccine dish ~ simple to prepare, rich and delicious. Cooked, crumbled bacon folded in or on top gives it more colour and flavour.

ingredients

ALFREDO sauce:

2 Tbsp. butter
1½ cups 35% cream
2 cloves garlic, crushed
2 oz. white wine
1 oz. parsley, chopped
2 shallots, chopped

4 cups cooked noodles
Whole spring onion for garnish (optional)

directions

Melt 2 Tbsp. butter in a 4 quart saucepan. Sauté onions and garlic until transparent (about 2 minutes). Pour in white wine, add chopped parsley and stir to mix well. Add 4 cups cooked noodles (see Fettuccine di Mare recipe for instructions) and cream. Toss well. Garnish with whole spring onion if desired and serve.

note:

Pasta, like potatoes, rice and bread, is high in essential carbohydrates and vitamins needed in a regular diet. 1 cup of cooked noodles has only 106 calories.

Makes 4 servings ~ 571 calories per serving

Roast Prime Rib of Beef

When you're shopping for Prime Rib, try to buy the first and second ribs. They're the most tender, have the least fat and marbling, and the largest "eye" portion. Allow 8 ounces of meat per serving.

Yorkshire pudding

1 cup flour, ¼ tsp. salt, 1 cup milk, 2 eggs

Mix thoroughly and refrigerate, covered

to prepare roast

Preheat oven to 400°. Season roast with salt and pepper, and place fat side up in roasting pan with carrots, celery and onions (whole or diced). Roast uncovered in centre of oven for 20 mins. to seal in juices. Reduce heat to 325° and continue cooking for 1 hour, for medium "doneness". Remove from oven and let stand ½ hour on warm stove to allow juices to settle.

Meanwhile, return oven temperature to 400° for Yorkshire Pudding. Pour into each large muffin tin 1 Tbsp. of fat from roasting pan. Heat thoroughly in oven. Pour in batter to depth of ¾" and bake for ½ hour. Serve with roast beef.

to prepare 'au jus'

Remove ½ of the fat from roasting pan. Add 1 cup water in which 1 bouillon cube has been dissolved. Heat through on top element, stirring to mix. Add 1 Tbsp. flour if desired.

733 calories per serving

New York Steak

A good steak has always been one of the finer things in life. Topped with Maître d'Hôtel butter, it's a contender for the very best.

INGREDIENTS (Maître d'hôtel Butter)

This makes enough for 12 1-oz. servings and can be stored in the freezer for future gourmet steaks.

½ cup butter ~ 1 clove garlic, crushed ~ 2 Tbsp. lemon juice
1 oz. white wine ~ ½ oz. Worcestershire sauce ~ 1 oz. parsley

Soften butter and beat in remaining ingredients. Roll mixture in waxed paper, seal and freeze.

directions

To prepare 10 oz. New York ~ Cut centre steaks (1" thick): Preheat broiler. Season each steak lightly with freshly ground pepper and salt. Broil 3" from heat for: 4 minutes per side for "rare"; 5 minutes per side for "medium"; 6 minutes per side for "well~done".

When cooked as desired, place a 1 oz. slice of frozen butter on top of steak. Allow to melt and serve immediately.

note:
Serve steak with your choice of vegetables. We suggest: mushrooms, broccoli, cauliflower, carrots, or a tomato topped with Parmesan cheese and broiled golden brown.

660 calories per serving